Inspiring Unconditional Love 2

More
Reflections from the Heart

By

Harold W. Becker

White Fire Publishing

Inspiring Unconditional Love 2
More Reflections from the Heart

By Harold W. Becker

Copyright © 2011 Harold W. Becker

Published by:
White Fire Publishing
Tampa, Florida
www.whitefirepublishing.com

Cover Design and Interior Layout: John T. Goltz

Library of Congress Control Number: 2011923712

ISBN: 978-0-979046-05-6

First Printing: March 2011
Printed in the USA on acid free paper

Life is an amazing adventure of the heart.
Each moment is filled with limitless potential
and profound beauty when we come from the
awareness of love. These are the experiences
that bring true meaning to our lives and
encourage us to expand our love even more. It
is as simple as we make it.

Acceptance, both for ourselves and those
around us, is the key to living in joy and peace.
When we allow harmony and balance to
be our natural approach to life, we bring the
infinite spectrum of potential into focus. Using
our imagination, we create and manifest
incredible opportunities of love with each and
every heartbeat.

Embrace your dreams and engage your talents
as the world awaits your unique gifts. Infuse
your unconditional love with each breath and
as you share it, others will enjoy it with you.

Harold W. Becker

Inspiring Unconditional Love 2

More
Reflections from the Heart

Heart to heart we build a world filled with peace and harmony, love and prosperity.

The dawn of a new day always comes with
a fresh opportunity to create with love.

To love is to be.

Unconditional love extends the hand of friendship
since it already knows itself in the other.

Infinite potential is revealed in the
grace of a single heartbeat.

For every momentary thought of fear there is
an eternity of love waiting to be expressed.

When we step back from our perceived
challenges, the presence of love becomes clear.

Through love you become
intimate with the infinite.

Yesterday was beautiful and tomorrow will be too,
just by being love right now you are truly you.

Beyond the limitations of the mind is
your heart waiting to be explored.

Begin within.

The simplest act of kindness
changes countless lives.

We all share the innate and eternal
freedom to love unconditionally.

Let each breath be filled with love today.

One love connects us all.

There is more power and potential
in a single expression of love than
a lifetime of accumulated fear.

Love is present even during
moments when we are not.

There is amazing beauty in every heart and
your compassion reveals it's potential.

Let this moment be one of unconditional love.

Love enjoys the journey while being
present right where it is.

Unconditional love embraces all that is
and encourages all that can be.

The joy of living comes from the
love you are sharing.

With each loving thought, feeling,
word, and action, we breathe new
life into our beautiful world.

Love who you are and you will always
know who loves you - love others as they
are and they will know your love.

When you are present in love,
solutions are obvious.

In moments of fear just remember
love is always here.

Love is simply the awareness
of who you really are.

Patience, compassion, trust, and wisdom are
all qualities of living life from your heart.

The love that flows through you flows to you.

Unconditional love is without beginning or
end, exists everywhere and found nowhere,
is never proven yet instantly known.

Release all that no longer serves you and
allow the love that you are to shine.

With each and every heartbeat
you are love made manifest.

A simple way to start each day... "I
love myself unconditionally!"

A passion for compassion comes
from an awakened heart.

Fear lasts as long as you focus on it, love lasts an eternity as it focuses through you.

While our mind wanders in search of love, our heart knows exactly where it is.

Love breathes life into every moment allowing us to create and expand more love.

Think outside the box and feel the circle of life.

When you share your love your acts
of kindness will never be random.

Feel the love from your heart and your smile
will be spontaneous and contagious.

A quiet mind and an open heart reveal
the beauty and perfection of life.

Simply embrace the miracle of love that you are.

Love is your eternal essence
flowing through you now.

We realize love as our real eyes love.

It is the unconditional nature of love
that often confounds the mind while
bringing joy to the heart.

Boundless and beautiful, you are an
exquisite and radiant presence of love.

Be the love that is the center of your being.

Love knows what the mind forgets.

The love you seek is the love you already are.

To become conscious of unconditional love,
begin with loving yourself unconditionally.

The broader our view, the more we
realize love is always present.

Your unconditional love awakens and
encourages the love in those around you.

The more you love, the more you love.

Love is the simple solution to all the
seemingly complicated problems of life.

The miracle of love is its eternal presence.

Whatever you choose next, infuse
love and your decision will instantly
encompass the greatest good of all.

As a being of love, you are a
treasure beyond measure.

Fear is only a momentary raincloud
to the love that is always shining.

A new world emerges when you
embrace life with love.

The love shared today inspires
a beautiful tomorrow.

Life does not labor over love, it
simply loves unconditionally.

Love always finds its way from heart to heart.

Unconditional love knows no equal
yet embraces all equally.

To walk the journey of love with another
is to enjoy the reflection of love itself.

Beauty is obvious to all those
that live from their heart.

Live the simple life of love.

We thank you precious earth for your
unconditional love and endless sustenance.

The love of One is the love of All.

Your loving presence on this earth is more
brilliant than the light of a thousand suns
and the sparkle of a galaxy of stars.

In the heart of love one finds
the wisdom of the ages.

Love is here so there is nothing to fear.

Your unconditional love is the seed of
potential for others to blossom.

Your peace builds world peace.

Your courage to love gives others
the experience of love.

As we fall in love today we spring forth in joy.

A full heart and a quiet mind
inspire infinite possibilities.

Know love and you will have no doubt.

As a loving presence, you reveal and
inspire beauty in each moment.

Your brilliant love casts no shadows.

The heart leads to new adventures
while the mind enjoys the path.

A hug brings two hearts together as one.

Observe with compassion rather
than judge with condemnation.

Alive with love we truly live.

Your love inspires love.

The presence of love is eternally
present within you.

Joy is the expression of your heart
radiating love for life.

Love is the essence of who you are and the
creative potential of all that you desire to become.

Love the world you were born to create.

Trust your choices and you will
love your experiences.

Unconditional love... it really is that simple.

Beyond our limited perceptions and
beliefs are new worlds to explore.

We literally transform life when we share our love.

Love is a beautiful journey of self
discovery and universal expression.

Beyond our accepted beliefs, habits,
and rituals is the simplicity of love.

A choice of love inspires life itself
to unfold in new ways.

The essence of eternity is the love
expressed in the moment.

Forgiveness releases the limitations
we have placed on love.

Love never withholds love.

The greatest strength comes from the softest heart.

Love cherishes the moment as it anticipates
the next heartbeat of potential.

Gratitude for life is being fully in love with life.

Love prospers through you.

Be your own best friend and you
will have a friend for life.

Gentle and kind is a loving state of mind.

Love encourages the realization of
our highest hopes and dreams.

Sing your solo of love rather
than in a choir of fear.

Nature's beauty and diversity reminds
us of the love we so often forget.

Each time we hug one another we
touch generations with our love.

A simple smile from a loving
heart initiates more smiles.

The mind often wanders while the
heart remains forever in love.

Your love shines with compassion.

Even the hardest heart has a spark of love
that grows with your soft embrace.

Love needs no words as it is the
universal language from the heart.

Love endures what our mind demurs.

Our true abundance is love of which
we all have an infinite supply.

Beautiful, loving, courageous, creative
and wise is the true you.

Observe life from a larger perspective
and love becomes obvious.

Our attention upon love expands
our presence of love.

Fear is only a forgotten moment that we are love.

The love you share now becomes part
of your past and your future.

From this breath to the next, all is well.

Love inspires greatness that benefits all.

To be yourself, let others be.

You bring out the love in others
by knowing your own love.

Whatever you may wish to be or do is only
a tiny fragment of who you already are.

The heart of life is in you.

The wisdom of the heart outshines
the knowledge of the mind.

Know love within and you will never be without.

The joy of eternity is found in the
presence of love right now.

Each heartbeat sustains trillions of cells,
imagine what one thought of love can do.

Gratitude is the natural expression
when we come from our heart.

Appreciate the countless gifts in life
as they are all given in love.

We give thanks because we can.

Love with wisdom is our personal power.

No matter how deep the pain,
love always remains.

Our love touches countless lives and
inspires destinies of greatness.

Encourage others to follow their
heart as you follow yours.

Unconditional love is the cosmic
glue that unites me and you.

The mind seeks while the heart knows.

Our opinions are nothing compared to our love.

When we choose to love without condition
we are fulfilling our life's purpose.

The warmth of your heart
radiates comfort to others.

Unconditional love releases the judgment
of right and wrong, good or bad.

Love is the simplest effort with
the most profound effect.

The love you share is wealth beyond measure.

A peaceful mind and loving heart cultivates
a loving mind and peaceful heart.

Change is a beautiful unfolding of
the everlasting nature of love.

Love is a priceless gift you can give
anytime, anywhere, to anyone.

Love illuminates potentials,
possibilities and solutions.

The love that dances in our heart
brings joy to our world.

Embrace what was, enjoy what is,
and imagine what will be.

Unconditional love is inclusive and
universal, intimate and personal.

A genuine life is built on a foundation of love.

Love is never proven yet is known
beyond any doubt.

We demonstrate our love by
the way we live our life.

The spark of love is in each of
us, we choose to ignite it.

Your presence is the essence of love
made tangible in this world.

When you hug another, you
experience the embrace too.

The smallest gesture of kindness can
change the destiny for many.

Love inspires creation.

Laughter lightens life.

Neither an idol nor an ideal, love
is simply a way of being.

Peace and joy are gifts from a loving heart.

Love continues on its journey
long after we share it.

Begin with loving yourself and you
will find no end to your love.

Each moment is a gift of love giving
birth to new potentials.

Our universal family is united through love.

Logic defines while love simply designs.

Love transcends the cycles of life.

With unconditional love, every
moment is a new beginning.

Our five senses pale in comparison
to our awareness of love.

What we resist in fear is easily
embraced with love.

Love is ever present, we are the ones
that either trust or deny it.

A simple gaze into the night sky reminds
us how truly infinite love is.

Fear repels whereas love invites.

To love when it is most challenging
is to understand love.

When we love, we assist the
world right where we are.

Love does not depend on words as it
is readily felt from heart to heart.

Earth is born anew with the love
that comes from you.

Love is our gift to others rather than an
awaited response from another.

Look with your heart into the mirror of life
and you will see love reflecting back.

Joy is the peaceful stillness of mind
and the heart overflowing.

Love evolves what fear revolves.

The dreams of love from our heart
manifest in our world.

Compassion appreciates what is
rather than judges what is not.

With each heartbeat we are granted a
fresh potential to share our love.

Radiant and spectacular, you are
the one who knows love.

No matter how far our mind may
wander, our heart is always with us.

Like the merging colors of the rainbow,
our love blends with those around us.

Sharing love brings more of it into our lives.

We nourish and flourish with love.

The complexity of life is resolved
in the simplicity of love.

The love from our heart is the
compassion we impart.

Love needs no reason to love.

World peace begins with your peace.

Loving earth is as vital as loving ourselves.

Although seemingly silent and invisible,
love is profound and obvious.

Although seemingly silent and invisible,
love is profound and obvious.

The physiological aspects of love are like
experiencing a single star in a universe of love.

Love your imagination for it is the
heart of your creativity.

Embrace today for it comes to you
as a gift filled with opportunity.

Life breathes to the rhythm of love.

Doubt and fear are simply moments
of forgetting our love.

Balance in life begins within.

Love trusts us even when we do not trust love.

Each of us has the power to change the
world, imagine what we can do together.

When we open our heart to others,
we allow others into our heart.

Self acceptance is the first step
to accepting others.

Gratitude is more than an attitude; it is a
knowing that love is always flowing.

Embrace what you resist and it will
transform into what you accept.

The infinite is filled with love and it is all infinite.

Love's compassion is our common passion.

Kindness creates more kindness as
these ripples of love touch others.

To know where love begins, look within.

We will never know love if we are afraid to love.

Generosity is sharing from a full heart.

Judgment divides while love simply guides.

The intelligence of our intricate physical body is a miracle in itself and that is just one example.

A brilliant mind is nothing compared to a loving heart, yet together they are true wisdom.

Diversity encourages unique creativity rather than conformity.

Fear may motivate a momentary response while love inspires a lifetime.

The very nature of love is to give of
itself in order to expand more love.

Love is priceless and infinite and already yours.

True love is boundless and real
without limitation or imitation.

With the awareness of love comes limitless
potential and profound beauty.

Begin each new day with a blank canvas and
paint your reality with dreams from the heart.

Nature understands and embodies
unconditional love.

Life and love are happening right now.

Our precious earth is a living
example of love for all life.

Knowing who we are is not enough if we do
not remember that we are a part of it all.

Consciously and lovingly embracing
change is how we evolve.

Our love is what gives a deeper meaning to life
and makes it easy, joyful and unconditional.

There is magnificent beauty all around us
when we choose to observe life through love.

Amazing wisdom is right within us when
we are patient and listen to our heart.

Gentleness and kindness are innate
natural resources that benefit all.

Love is exquisitely simple.

With diversity comes incredible opportunity.

Living each moment with love is to
be healthy, wealthy and wise.

Love is the key that unlocks our
greatest possibilities.

The ideas we entertain in our consciousness
are the seeds of a future yet to be made.

Listening to our heart brings the infinite
spectrum of potential into focus.

Choosing a loving and affirming
perspective manifests this as our reality.

Recognize the splendor held within each
moment and you understand love.

Our love is powerful beyond
our wildest imagination.

Love is infinite and intended to
be shared unconditionally.

We create and manifest incredible opportunities
of love with each and every heartbeat.

Your brilliance is only veiled by limited beliefs;
your light shines eternally bright within.

As weavers of love, we are also intricately
woven into the very fabric of life itself.

Love is always present even in the moments
we forget love is always present.

Joy is the song of the heart.

Self acceptance is the basis to
inner joy and peace.

We bring a unique element to universal creation
with our conscious awareness of love.

Embrace the dreams of your heart for
the world awaits your unique gifts.

Lead by the example of love and
you walk together with all.

This is your precious moment to enjoy love.

Notice every good thing in your life and you realize the treasure you already have.

From our very first breath we are filled with limitless love and universal potential.

The full expression of love resides
in the present moment.

Love endures the most difficult
circumstances and still remains as love.

Change is constant whereas love never changes.

Our unrealized potential is only limited
by the beliefs we cling to about life.

Life is experienced as joy or struggle
according to which perspective we choose.

Every moment of every day we have a choice to
be love… whether we are conscious of it or not.

Sharing our love provides new
opportunities presently undreamed of.

Everything becomes lighter and brighter
through a simple act of self acceptance.

Our innermost desires come from
our heart, not our intellect.

It is, and always has been, our choice to
embrace the love that resides within.

Emerge into each new day ready
to create in a new way.

Your presence makes a profound difference
simply because there will never be another you.

A healthy life starts first and foremost
with acceptance and love for self.

The heart speaks through intuition
as it guides us with love.

Like a bud coming into bloom, love unfolds
from within to express our true beauty.

The simplicity and intricacy of love defies logic
and gives meaning to the word elegance.

When we release the past with love a
whole new life opens up before us.

We all share a common, universal bond
of amazing potential through love.

Where there is love there is no
lack and love is everywhere.

Love is like a precious tapestry that unites
us in our diverse interconnectedness
and interdependence.

Words are energized by love or hate; one
appreciates while the other separates.

Life is a dance driven by the
rhythm of the heartbeat.

Peace is found in the tranquility
of unconditional love.

Each of us is endowed with the pure essence
of love at the very center of our being.

In the stillness of your heart you
will find a symphony of love.

Your intention to love leads the way to more love.

Unconditional love is an unlimited way of being.

Our children are the reminders
of the love we often forget.

Even though we feel secure in the known, it is the
unknown that holds real potential and possibility.

Our life story is written with love
and told from the heart.

From the deepest pain to the greatest joy,
unconditional love simply accepts it all.

To embrace a seeming mistake is to understand
that all things are expressions of love.

Unconditional love knows no duality
and therefore creates no problems.

Your energy flows freely with love and is
restricted by anything less than love.

Love has nothing to defend
and everything to give.

Our senses crudely interpret what
our heart already knows.

On wings of love we take flight,
soaring above duality.

Each spoken word from the heart is a
soothing balm of healing love.

When we appreciate what is, life naturally
brings us even more to appreciate.

Our internal insights shed light on
our external experiences.

Brilliant and true is the heart of beautiful you.

Love is real strength and courage.

Life is yours to live just as love is yours to give.

When we are childlike we dance with life itself.

You are loved unconditionally.

About the Author

Harold W. Becker has dedicated his life to understanding, living and sharing unconditional love. In 1990 he formed his consulting company, Internal Insights, and in 2000 he founded the non-profit, The Love Foundation, Inc., with the mission of "inspiring people to love unconditionally."

In his desire to touch the world with this timeless message of love, Harold conceived Global Love Day, an international celebration of humanity, held annually each May 1st.

He is the author of several additional books including, *Internal Power: Seven Doorways to Self Discovery, Unconditional Love – An Unlimited Way of Being, Unconditional Love Is... Appreciating Aspects of Life, and Inspiring Unconditional Love - Reflections from the Heart.* He also wrote and hosted his own PBS television special program entitled, *Unconditional Love – A Guide to Personal Freedom* available on DVD.

Harold has an MBA and enjoys bringing his inspirational and motivational vision into every facet of his life including his business activities, writing, speaking, seminars and consulting. Blending incredible insight and intuition with humor, compassion and kindness, he encourages people to love unconditionally.

You can reach Harold through the following web sites:
www.internalinsights.com
www.thelovefoundation.com
www.globalloveday.com
www.whitefirepublishing.com